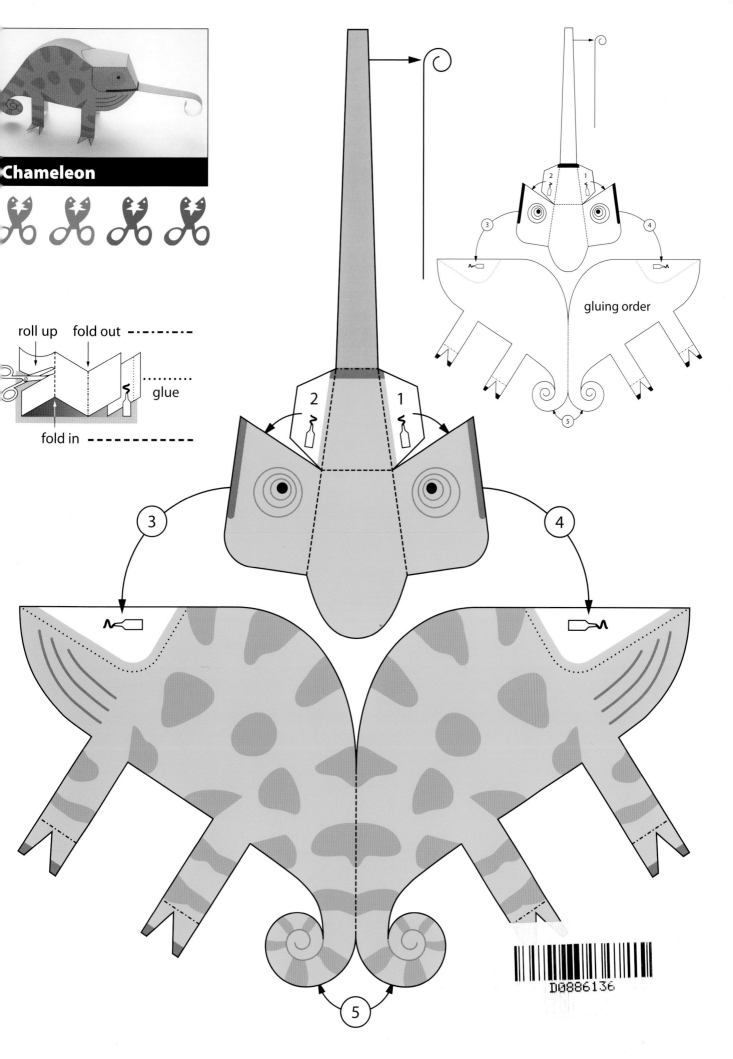

Chameleon

roll up
fold out · — · — · — ·
. . . .
glue
fold in — — — —

gluing order

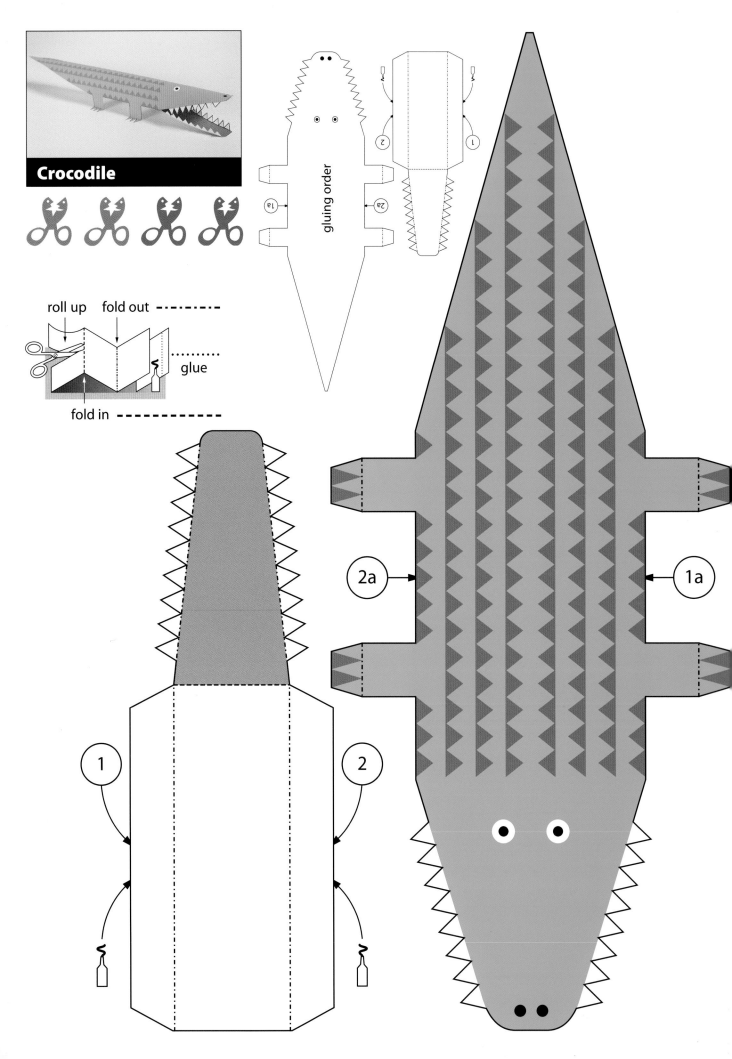

Crocodile

roll up
fold out ·—·—·—·—

fold in ·—·—·—·—

glue ·············

gluing order

1
2

1a
2a

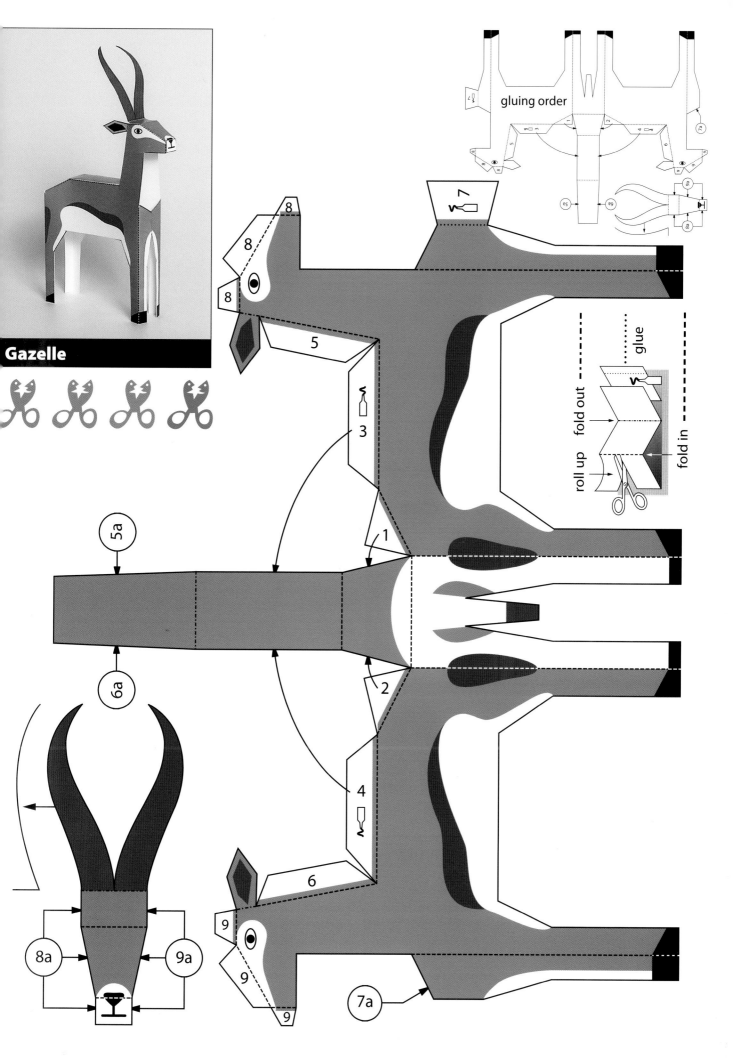

Gazelle

gluing order

fold out / roll up / glue / fold in

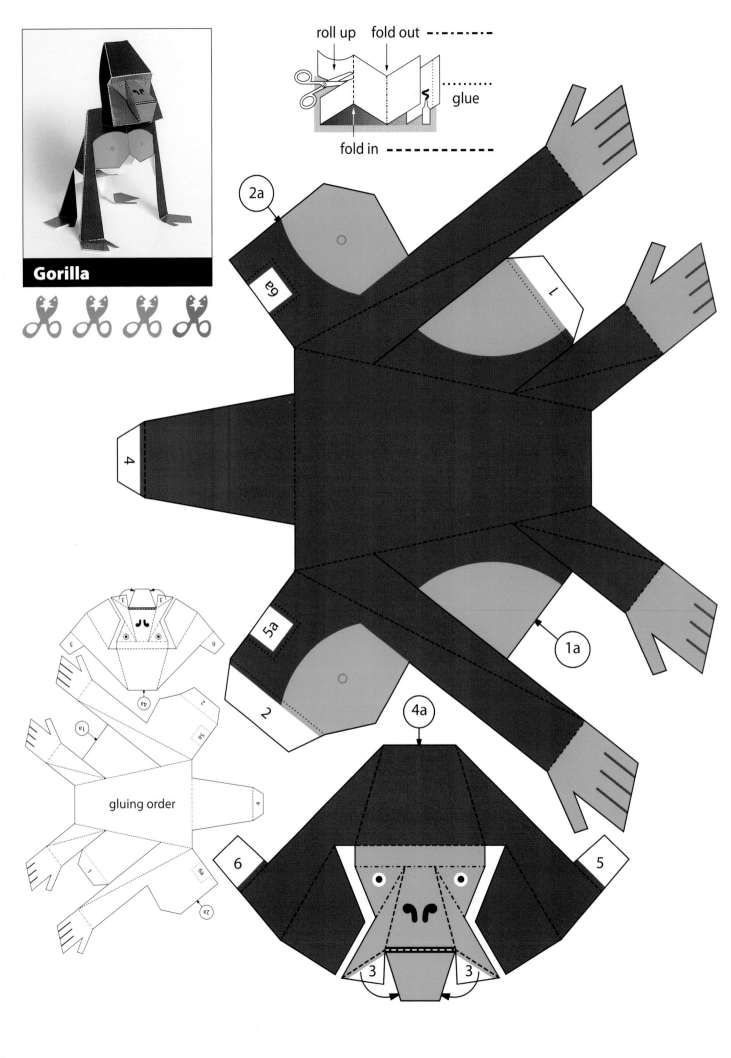

Gorilla

roll up   fold out ·—·—·—·—

glue

fold in ·—·—·—·—

gluing order

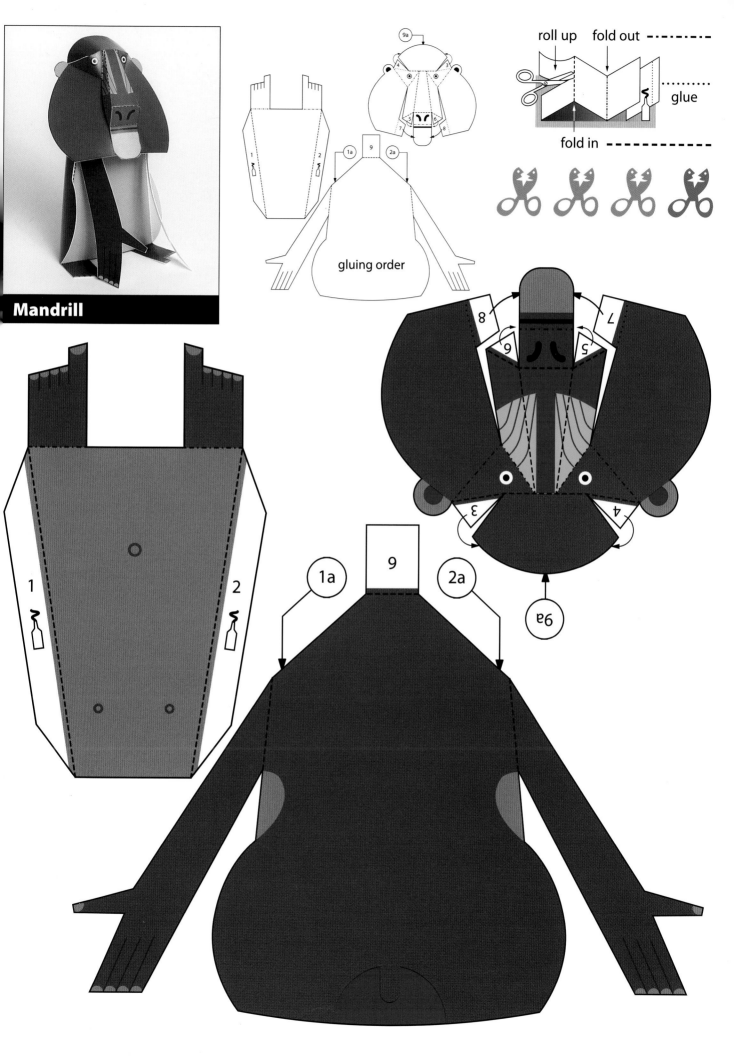

Mandrill

roll up   fold out   - · - · - · -

glue

fold in   - - - - - -

gluing order

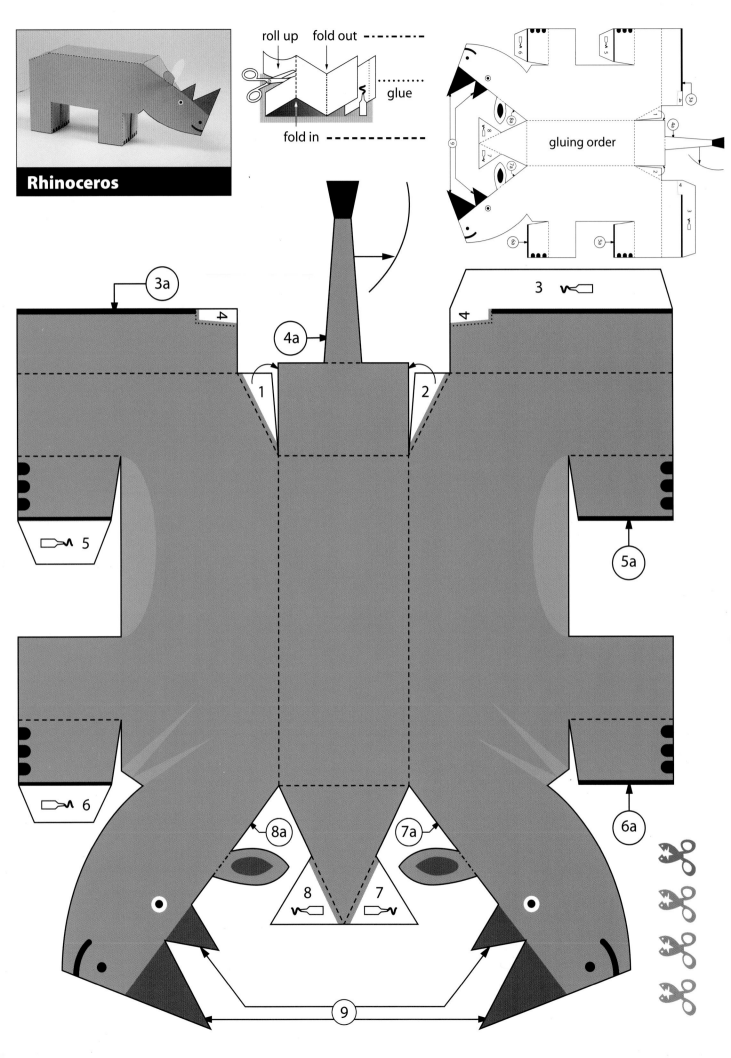

Rhinoceros

roll up   fold out — ·· — ·· —

glue ········

fold in — — — — —

gluing order

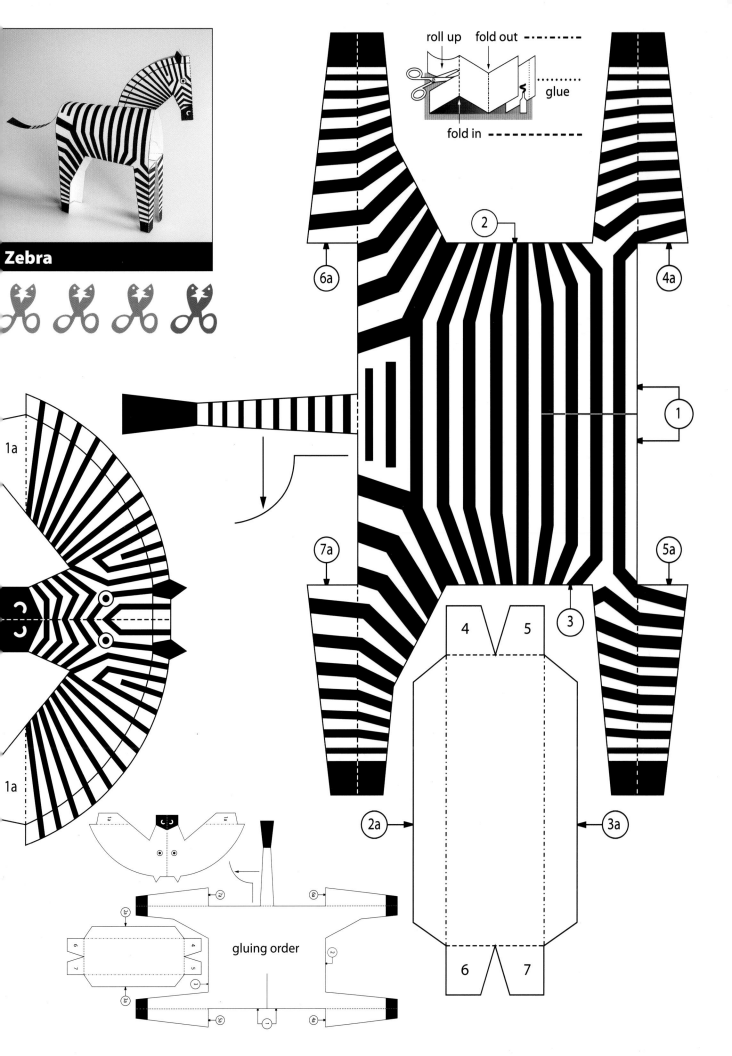

Zebra

roll up · fold out - · - · - · -
glue ········
fold in - - - - - - - - -

gluing order

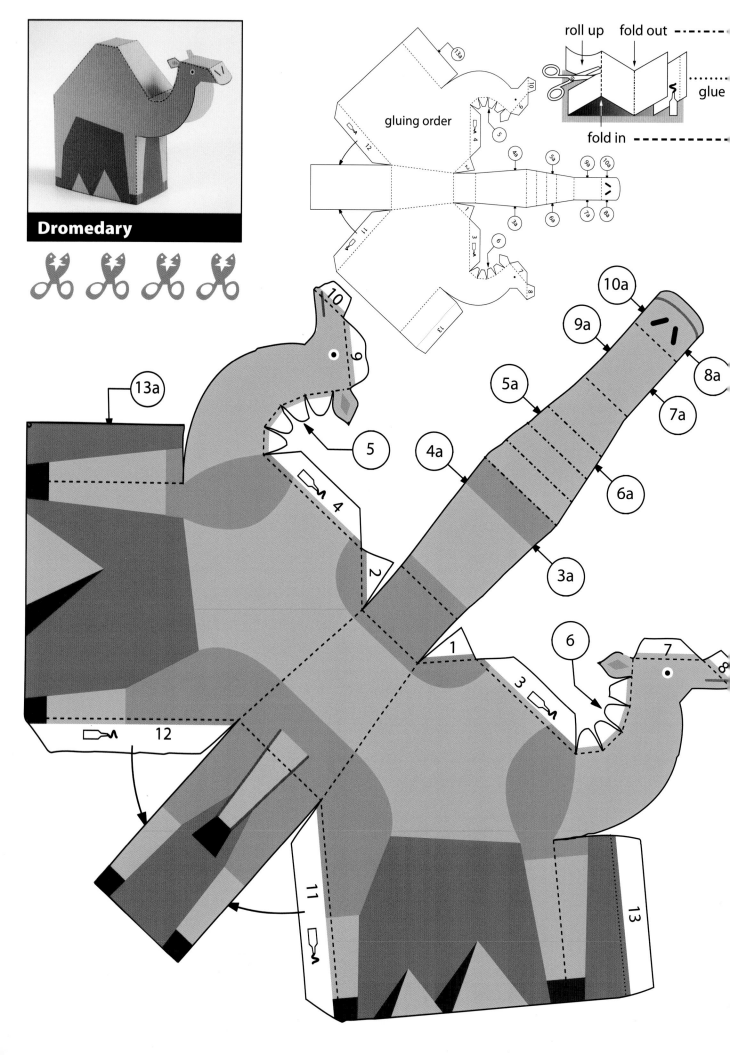

Dromedary

roll up fold out ------
glue
fold in ------

gluing order

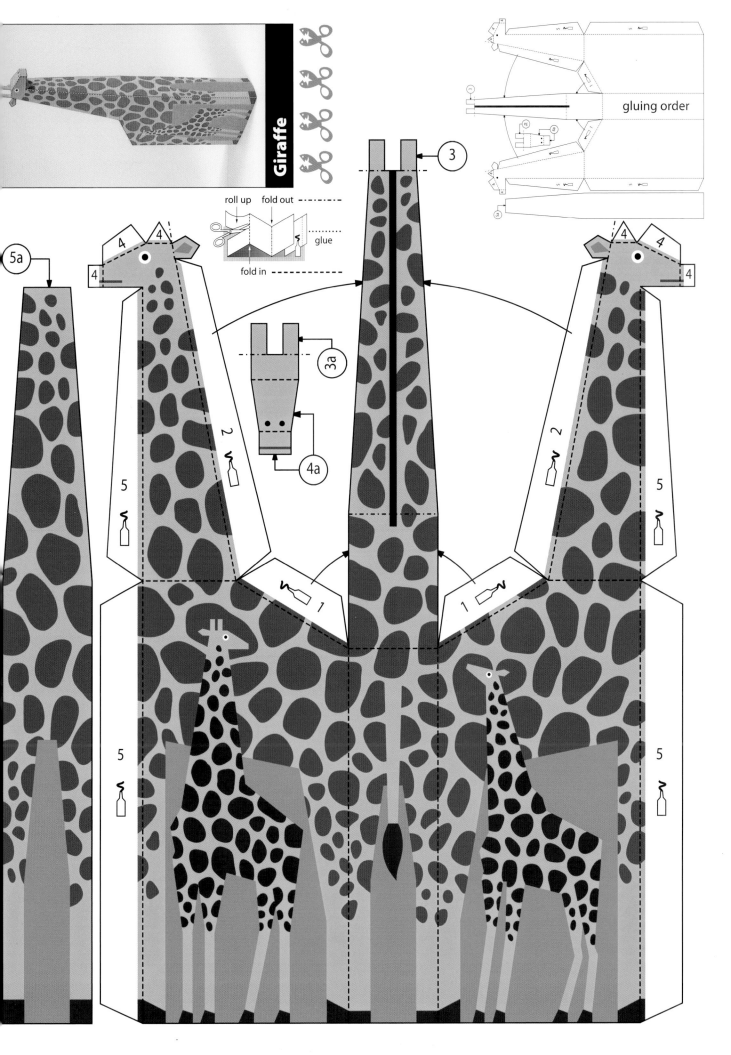

Giraffe

gluing order

roll up   fold out ·─·─·─·
                          glue ....
fold in   ─ ─ ─ ─ ─

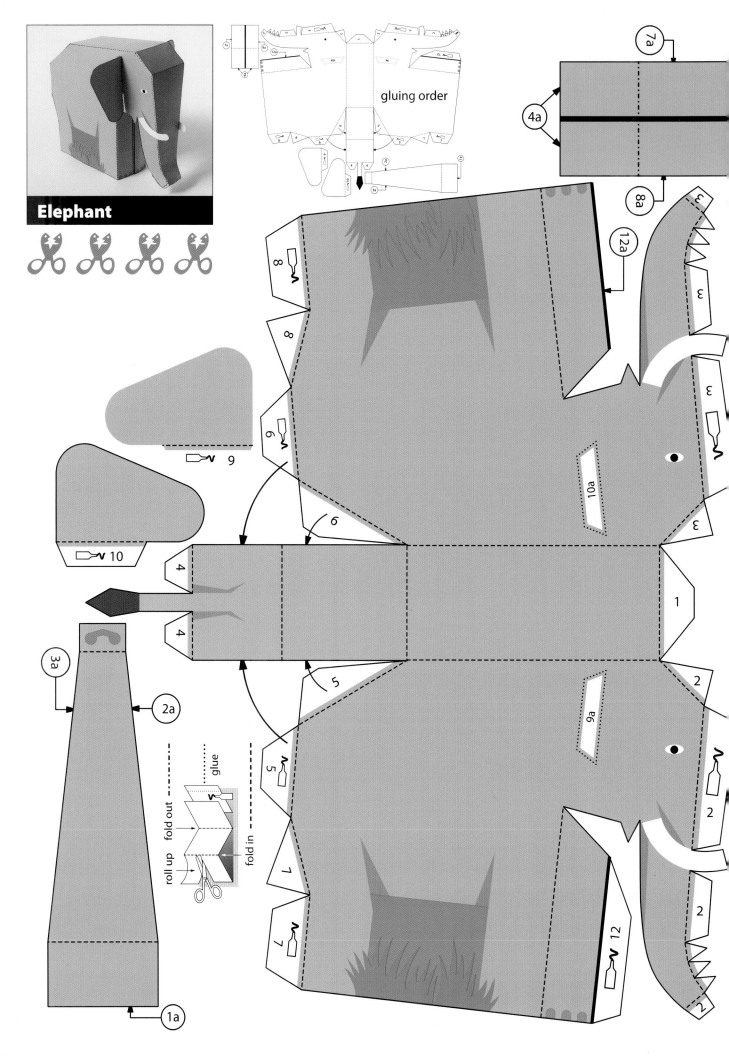

Elephant

gluing order

glue
fold out
roll up
fold in

Hippopotamus

roll up

fold out ---·---·---

········· glue

fold in - - - - - - -

gluing order

1

5   6

8   7

2

3   4

6a   7a

1a

5a   8a

9

10

3a   4a

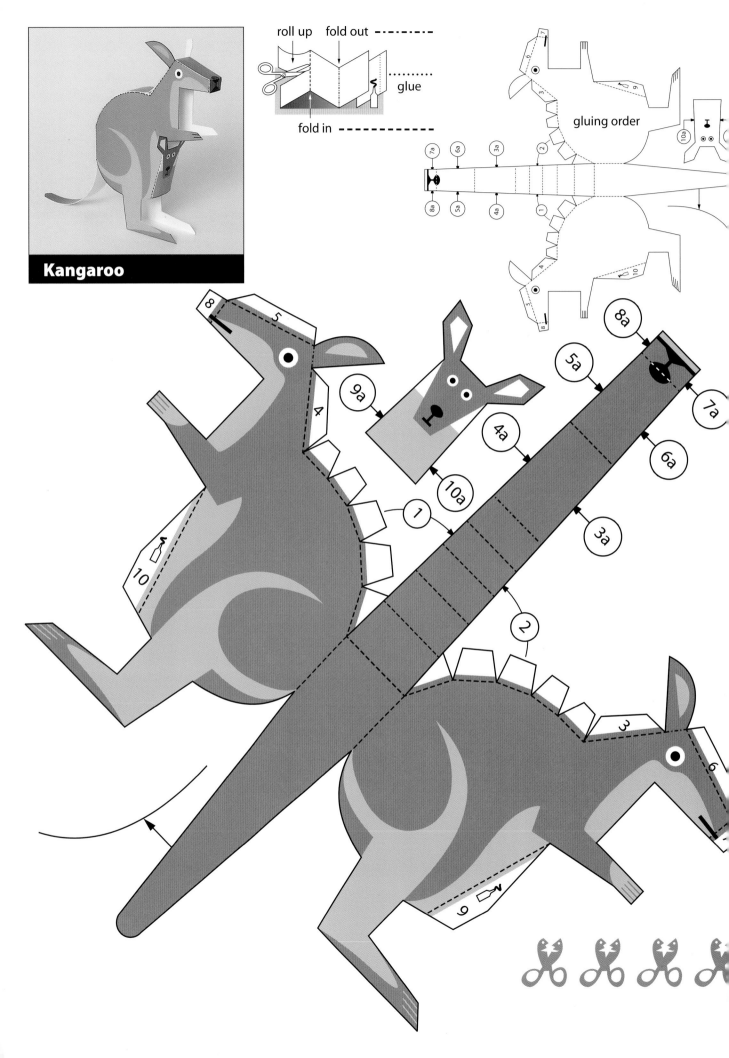

Kangaroo

roll up   fold out ‑‑‑‑‑‑‑‑
fold in ‑‑‑‑‑‑‑‑‑‑‑‑
glue ‑‑‑‑‑‑‑‑‑‑

gluing order